$8.99

Praise
In Many Colors

HYMNS,
SPIRITUALS,
GOSPEL SONGS,
AND CAROLS

D1611495

ARRANGED FOR SOLO PIANO
by Melody Bober

Lillenas PUBLISHING COMPANY

KANSAS CITY, MO 64141

C O N T E N T S

A Mighty Fortress Is Our God

MARTIN LUTHER
Arr. by Melody Bober

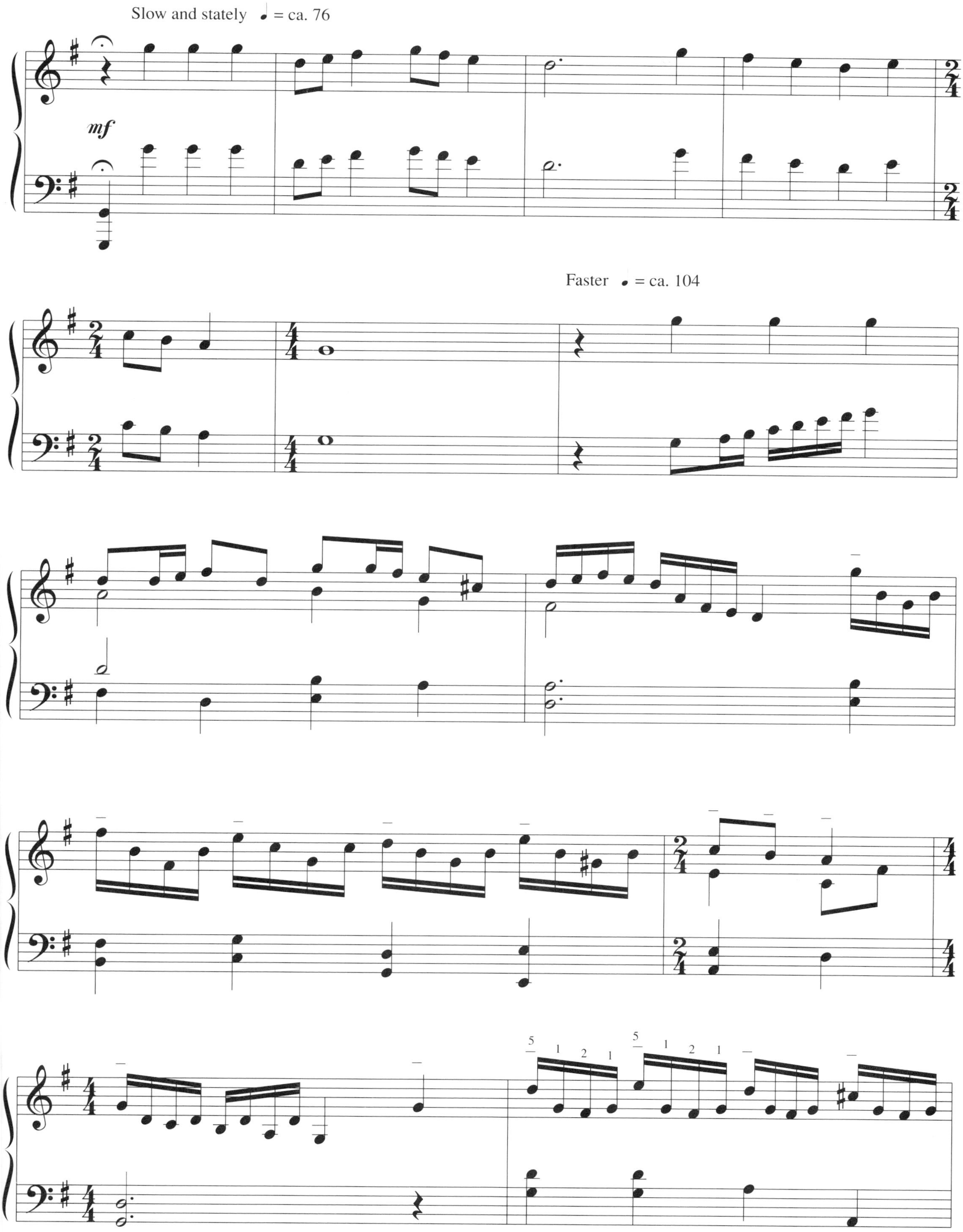
Slow and stately ♩ = ca. 76
mf
Faster ♩ = ca. 104
5 1 2 1 5 1 2 1

10

12

Spiritual Medley

Rock-a My Soul
He's Got the Whole World in His Hands
Swing Low, Sweet Chariot
Joshua Fit the Battle of Jericho

With energy   ♩ = ca. 76

Arr. by Melody Bober

"Rock-a My Soul" (Spiritual)

"He's Got the Whole World in His Hands" (Spiritual)

mp

"Swing Low, Sweet Chariot" (Spiritual)

Swing feel ♩ = ca. 70

Suddenly faster ♩ = ca. 92   "Joshua Fit the Battle of Jericho" (Spiritual)

rit.

8vb

mp

In My Heart There Rings a Melody

ELTON M. ROTH
Arr. by Melody Bober

decresc. and rall.

mf

8vb 8vb

Slower, rubato

f

Like chimes, heavy pedal

Broad

8vb 8vb 8vb

accel. little by little to the end

Hark! Medley

Hark! the Herald Angels Sing
Angels We Have Heard on High
God Rest Ye Merry, Gentlemen

Arr. by Melody Bober

Bright ♩ = ca. 120

"Hark! the Herald Angels Sing" (Felix Mendelssohn)

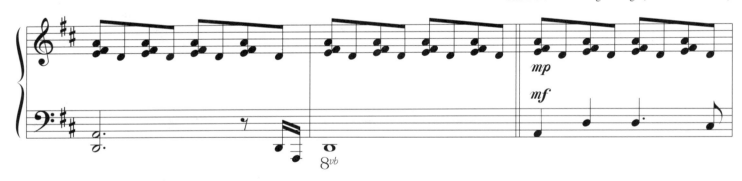

"Angels We Have Heard on High" (Trad. French Melody)

"God Rest Ye Merry, Gentlemen" (English Melody)

All Hail the Power of Jesus' Name

OLIVER HOLDEN
Arr. by Melody Bober

Energetically ♩ = ca. 108

Old Time Religion

Spiritual
Arr. by Melody Bober

38

Joy to the World

GEORGE FREDERICK HANDEL
Arr. by Melody Bober

The Old Rugged Cross

GEORGE BENNARD
Arr. by Melody Bober

46

The First Noel

17th Century English Carol
Arr. by Melody Bober

Rubato ♩ = ca. 88

54

When the Roll Is Called Up Yonder

JAMES M. BLACK
Arr. by Melody Bober

Whiter than Snow

Delicately ♩ = ca. 96

WILLIAM G. FISCHER
Arr. by Melody Bober

64

67

Glorious Things of Thee Are Spoken

FRANZ JOSEPH HAYDN
Arr. by Melody Bober

Broad and majestic ♩. = 58

I Saw Three Ships

Traditional
Arr. by Melody Bober